Escape
from
Jersey City

Escape
from
Jersey City

George J. Searles

Clare Songbirds
Publishing House

Clare Songbirds Publishing House Poetry Series
ISBN 978-1-957221-28-1
Clare Songbirds Publishing House
Escape from Jersey City© 2025 George J. Searles

Printed in the United States of America
FIRST EDITION

140 Cottage Street
Auburn, New York 13021
www.claresongbirdspub.com

To Ellis

Acknowledgements:
Many of these poems were originally published (or have been accepted) by print and online magazines:

The Alembic: Discretion
Ariel Chart: Homage to Leon Golub
Brillig: A Load off My Mind, Perfect Timing
Café Review: Cultural Differences, One Nite Only: Free
    Beer & Chicken
California Quarterly: Customer Service Has Its Limits, The
    Fortune Teller's Bad Day
Chiron: Playground
Chronogram: Big, Beefy Guys with Pony Tails, Guitar
    Lessons, "If" Is a Big Word, Midnight, Overheard at
    the Diner, Post Mortem, Three Questions, and Willie,
    Mickey, & the Duke
    Concho River Review: On Good Authority
    Creosote: His Master's Vice
Evening Street Review: Much Obliged, U.S. Government
    Printing Office and Workplaces from Hell
Fern: Fatal Distraction
Gargoyle: Shoptalk
Home Planet News: Governing Wisely, In My Next Life,
    and Smooth Talker
Iconoclast: Incentive
Krax: Adverse Reactions
Light: Starter Resartus
Madswirl: Everything's Under Control
Main Street Rag: Civil Service and Leave Well Enough Alone-
Misfit Magazine: Husserl's Phenomenology
Molecule: At Sea
Muse: Higher Education
Nut House: Science
The Potomac: Avoiding Unsafe Sex
Rattle: The First Annual AHS Wipeout 5K Run
The Raven's Perch: My Cousin Vinny, Selective Enforcement
Red Rock Review: The Has-Been
Rockford Review: Lieutenant Columbo's Wife
Rye Whiskey Review: La Cerveza Mas Fina
Seneca Review: Back in the 20th Century We Kept Ourselves
    Pretty Busy
Slab: Semper Paratus
Taproot: Mixed Blessing
Third Wednesday: Advice to the Crows

Time of Singing: Fall Term
Trajectory: Coming Soon, False Advertising, Progress, Pulling
    the Rabbit Out of the Hat, Retirement, and Six? I'm Impressed,
Words & Images: Missing

Any merit in my poems is largely attributable to the influence of the many excellent poets whose workshops I've enjoyed so much over the years: Jeanne Marie Beaumont, Star Black, the late Lucie Brock-Broido, Christopher Citro, Billy Collins, Wyn Cooper, the late Robert Creeley, Carol Muske Dukes, the late Stephen Dunn, Doug/Diana Goetsch, Stephanie Hart, Marie Howe, Susan Kinsolving, the late Thomas Lux, David Mason, Campbell McGrath, Heather McHugh, Honor Moore, Sharon Olds, the late Len Roberts, Vijay Seshadri, Julie Sheehan, Dave Smith, Michael Waters, and Robert Wrigley.

Contents

I

Advice to the Crows

Hey, Guys. Take it from me:
You're handling this roadkill

routine all wrong (swooping down,
grabbing a bite, then zooming away

and, I'm sure, getting nervous indigestion
along with those delicious crimson entrails).

Instead, do it *this* way: When you see
the squashed squirrel or squished kitty,

work together; pick it up, fly it over
to the side of the road, and feast in peace.

Much better, right? Of course.
But I don't expect you to listen.

I know from experience.
Nobody ever listens.

Six? I'm Impressed

Most of the time you can tell who's full
of shit and who's not, but you can never
know with absolute assurance, because,
Hey, it's not always completely clear-cut.

Take Jimmy the Uber driver, for instance.
One night at the bar—knowing I write poems—
he bragged, "Poems are fine, but I write novels."
"Really, Jim?" I asked, wondering if this

could possibly be true. "Yup," he answered,
downing another bottle of Bud Lite.
"I've written six novels—all pretty good!
Now all I have to do is type them up."

La Cerveza Mas Fina

Amy squinted at her phone and groaned.
"Jeez! It's almost noon already,
and I have to get up way early tomorrow!"

Of course, we all knew she meant *midnight*.
But scofflaw smoke was wafting overhead,
and our lovably madcap bartender was pouring

everyone free shots, and good old Mungo Jerry
was skiffling along on the jukebox, reminding us
that it was summertime, when the weather is fine,

and we'd all had a *lot* of Coronas by then.
So Amy's little error was understandable;
strict accuracy was not to be expected.

Another Argument for Vegetarianism

According to Christian mythology,
the 16th Century Carthusian monks abstained

from meat, and straightaway fell sound asleep
whenever it was served to them.

I know how embarrassed they must've felt,
having nodded off myself at the diner this morning

in front of my bacon & eggs "Lumberjack Breakfast"
after a long night of faith-based endeavor.

Next time, I'll be sure to order the tofu waffles
with a side of plant-based sausage maybe.

Fatal Distraction

Precocious little Sharon and I, in eighth grade,
enjoyed what passed back then for steamy romance
until one day in the schoolyard when some older kids
made fun of her for wearing "falsies." She fired back,

fearlessly, called them "God-damned son of a bitches,"
thereby earning yet another pair of distinctions:
the lead role in this poem, and historic status
as the first name on my grim roster of former flames.

In fact, she launched the list at that very moment,
because, even all those many years ago, I knew
I would never be content to spend the rest of my life
with a woman unable to pluralize correctly.

The Spanking Machine

Our Catholic school's tougher kids
swore on their mothers
that it had big, rusty nails
protruding from its paddles.
But we all knew this was bullshit.

Big, rusty nails? No way.
Not even the nuns would go *that* far.
I pictured it as sort of a mashup
of the Sing Sing electric chair
and the Gutenberg Press,

with plain wooden paddles poised
above the thick leather straps
designed to immobilize you,
bent over, pants down, shreiking
in fear, pain, and humiliation.

Whatever the machine really looked like,
it was in the basement somewhere,
back in the off-limits area
behind the bathrooms and janitor's shop,
and the long, spooky, unlit corridor

cluttered with cardboard storage boxes
piled like mummies in the catacombs or coffins
in the morgue. No one had actually seen it,
but we would've bet our lunch money
that it was there, though rarely used,

only for the most heinous offenses.
Really just once that we knew of for sure,
when that girl (Susan!) from the eighth grade
was expelled and never seen again.
Her offense became the stuff of legend.

The Has-Been

You've got to feel sorry for poor old Mr. F-bomb.
For years and years and years he was
The Man: a living legend—recognized,
everywhere respected, deferred to, lionized.

He had a big-time role to play:
CEO of profanity, you might well say.
But that was yesterday, and it's all just ancient
history now that Mr. F-bomb's been downsized.

Please do not misunderstand. The old guy's still around,
(and in his mind, at least) still kicking ass, still baaad.
But in truth his influence is so much less
than it once was, it's sad.

He's always coming in early,
working late, but for pocket change
and to no effect commensurate
with his WASP pedigree and stellar résumé.

Sure, he's free to come and go
all hours of the night and day.
But license can restrict; he's bored.
It's like a death-watch on the geriatric ward.

He's humored, condescended to,
just one more daft old toothless coot,
now that—see Kandinsky—alles really ist erlaubt
and the whole point of Carlin's list is moot.

No wonder Mr. F-bomb needs a drink!
He pushes through the dancehall's swinging doors.
His rusty spurs go "plinkle, clink"
and kick up puffs of sawdust from the floors.

But today all bets are off; we're a fourth of the way
into a whole new bloody siecle.
The unarmed man at the piano now
is not some scrawny, half-pint nervous wreck.

He does *not* abruptly stop the music,
grab his dorky little derby hat and scoot outside;
no, he just keeps right on playing funky stride,
ostinato, pretty much completely stoked on coke,

with no trace of fear. In fact, he's frisky.
Old F-bomb stands there backlit,
Clint Eastwood style, squinting through the smoke.
The bad guys barely glance up from their whiskey.

Much Obliged, U.S. Gov't Printing Office!
You Guys are the Best!

Take it from me: I'm one lucky customer,
with my brand-new consumer information catalog,

free of charge, from the Federal Citizen Information Center
in Pueblo, Colorado. Now I'll find out how to keep my heart
healthy,

discover twelve ways to lower my car insurance costs,
learn how to get an updated National Park System guide,

choose a cellular service, build a better credit record,
prevent food-borne illness, bone up on osteoporosis,

avoid foreclosure, select a new water heater, buy cheese,
prepare for retirement, plan my estate, and arrange my funeral.

Thanks to all the excellent booklets I'll order from my catalog,
I'll never have to worry about anything at all, ever again.

Starter Resartus

I want a Starter jacket
with a matching baseball hat,
and an Under Armour jersey
from the Jock Shoppe's high-priced rack.

My entire brand-new outfit
will have to be unique,
unlike most any other:
absolutely *fantastique*.

I want a striking uniform
that will set me right apart
as I shlep around the Super Mart
behind my shopping cart.

Any colors are acceptable
(except for Marlins teal),
but the overall effect...
well, it must have sex appeal.

Hey, it can be hometeam white
or even road-trip grey,
but the really most important thing
is what it has to say.

That's why the team-name logo
splashed bold across my back
cannot be some shopworn thing.
(We've had too much of that!)

So: No *Bosox* for this strutting dude,
no *Yankees, Giants*, or *Bucks*;
no *Flyers, Knicks*, or *Steelers*,
or any of those schmucks.

How about some European words
to make folks turn and stare?
Les Beaux Esprits, the coat could gloat,
or perhaps *Chargés d'Affaires*.

Or the logo could be something
based on literary shticks—
the *Joyceans* or *Pynchonites*
or, let's say, the *Moby Dicks*.

In any case, the whole point is
I must look like a mensch
in my macho All Star outfit,
not like one who rides life's bench.

The First Annual AHS Wipeout 5K Run

Believe it when I say this was a great day
for the American Hemorrhoids Society,
and for me. The race attracted hundreds
of socially conscious joggers and runners

from all over the area—each glad to fund-raise
for such a worthy cause and maybe achieve
at the same time a personal record on the fast,
straight, out & back course through town.

We showed up early and gathered in the park
near the starting line outside Sundown Vale
Assisted Living and exchanged the usual
self-congratulatory tales of recent performances,

and, of course, the predictable litany
of ailments: plantar fasciitis, sore knees,
the lower back issue, tendonitis, shin splints,
IBS—and yes, painful hemorrhoidal tissue.

According to these conversations, no one had trained
sufficiently, thereby providing a preemptive excuse
in case of a poor showing in the race, while some
of the faster kids and other reliable local standouts

did impressive wind sprints to loosen up and show off.
The event's sponsor, Preparation H, had a big truck
on site, decorated with the product's familiar logo,
and peppy young company reps wearing blue

and yellow T-shirts also bearing the logo were
giving away free samples. Some of us chose
to try them out right away, availing ourselves
of the porta potties arrayed on the sidewalk.

Then a tiny, clearly nervous girl from St. Jude's Pre-K
gamely labored through a quavering, slightly off-key
but well-received interpretation of the national anthem,
as we fidgeted patriotically and adjusted our watches.

Finally the starting gun was fired and we got moving, shuffling at first because of crowd congestion, but soon picked up speed as the pack thinned out. The weather that morning was cool and sunny, matching my mood.

I was flying, wings on my feet, the scenery a blur. Having just celebrated my 100th birthday, I was sure I'd finish well before lunch, first in my new age group, earning another of those coveted little plastic trophies.

Avoiding Unsafe Sex

Strolling around one sunny winter day
last year, I saw a mangy little mutt
intently humping a filthy snowbank.

He looked up and caught me watching,
and I could swear I heard him growl,
"What are *you* looking at, Chief?

"Go find your own action."
I considered this, but decided against it.
All the other snowbanks were filthy too.

Adding Insult to Injury

Wouldn't you know it? I come to my senses
and realize I'm lying on a heat grate
somewhere downtown on 7th Avenue,

totally butt-naked. Luckily,
nobody seems to care, or even notice.
(It's still New York, after all.)

Along comes this talking dog.
He tries to sell me a cheesy print
of *Whistler's Mother* (which I've never liked).

He has a whole stack of them piled high
in a little red wagon he's dragging around.
I figure I can sort of cover up with one

until some Good Samaritan happens by
with a terry cloth robe or a spare pair of gym shorts.
But I'm broke and the dog won't spot me the $9.99.

"Do I look like I was born yesterday?" he barks,
and trots away, tail in the air, leaving me
with an unobstructed view of his asshole.

Husserl's Phenomenology (Stanford UP, 2003)

On pg. 58 of this brief introductory study,
the author informs us that "One of the crucial
and much debated problems has been to specify

the relation between the object-as-it-is-intended
and the object-that-is-intended," and asks,
"Are we dealing with two quite different

ontological entities, or rather with two different
perspectives on one and the same?" A bit later
he ups the ante, inquiring "does the epoché imply

that we parenthesize the transcendent
spatio-temporal world in order to account
for internal mental representations,

or does the epoché rather imply
that we continue to explore and describe
the transcendent spatio-temporal world,

but now in a new and different manner?
Is the noema, the object-as-it-is-intended,
to be identified with an internal mental

representation—with an abstract and ideal
sense—or rather with the givenness
of the intended object itself?"

Dunno. Beats the shit outta me.

ONE NITE ONLY: Free Beer & Chicken

The Undertaker & His Pals,
The Barfly Harlots,
The Holland Daze Source,
The Roth/Updike Blues Band,
Time Ghost,
The Inca Pacitateds,
Three Dog Night,
The Dirty Elbows,
Phivestoopidlookinphux,
The Adirondack White Tail Dears,
Flight Risk,
The Doobie Brothers,
The Men in the White Coats,
The Swingin' Johnsons,
The Unruly Passengers,
Mott the Hoople,
Rialda and the Pissantics,
Those Stubborn Egg Stains,
Stone the Crow,
The Rez Erections.

Behind every great band
name, there's a story.

Perfect Timing, Literally

She was telling me
about her grandfather, who died
unexpectedly on September 10, 2001.

Actually a good thing, she explained,
because "he was super patriotic,
and if he'd seen 9/11,

it literally would've killed him."

Trouble in the Keystone State

The teams at James Buchanan High School
in Mercersburg, Pennsylvania, are nicknamed
The Blue Devils.

The teams at Mercersberg Academy
in Mercersberg, Pennsylvania, are nicknamed
The Blue Devils.

This may or may not be a Satanic plot,
but it does cause some confusion
on the *Mercersburg Journal* sports pages.

Maintaining Perspective

When the professor left his office
for a few minutes, he taped a note
to the door: "I'll be right back."

While he was gone, a student added,
"Who gives a shit?"
But let's look on the bright side.

The printing was neat and legible,
everything was spelled correctly,
and there was even a question mark.

All's Well That Ends Well

Remember the final scene in *Return of the Jedi*,
when the evil Emperor tortures young Luke Skywalker?

He tells Luke, "Complete your journey to the Dark Side."
But of course Luke's defiant, says "No way,"
or something to that effect, so the Emperor keeps
zapping him with little lightning bolts

that shoot from his outstretched fingers
into poor Luke's helpless, pain-wracked body,
twitching around on the floor of the observation deck:
Zap! Zap! Zap! Zap! Zap! Zap! Zap!

It's obvious the Emperor's getting off on this,
big time, leering obscenely at the effects of each jolt.
But the stalwart lad still refuses to give in,
so the Emperor zaps harder: ZAP! ZAP! ZAP! ZAP!

Though nearly half-dead, Luke remains obstinate,
and you can tell the Emperor's getting pissed now,
his pleasure giving way to frustration and rage
at our hero's bravery and fresh-faced fortitude.

Then Darth Vader, the Emperor's hulking right-hand man,
who's been watching all this, suddenly has a change
of heart, at least in part because he also happens to be
Luke's Dad—a far-fetched but convenient little detail.

He grabs the Emperor by the throat,
just as he'd done to a feckless underling
who'd screwed up somehow earlier in the film,
and throws him off the platform to his death.

Then he too dies, after doffing his respirator mask
so Luke can gaze upon his creepily pasty face.
And we must assume that, despite his lengthy rap sheet,
Lord Vader's finally saved by this last-ditch redemptive act.

It's all so reassuring…if you're about nine years old.

Baudrillard & Co.

What would sly Jean now have to say
if he were still alive today?

And how about famed Jacques Lacan,
not to mention Paul de Man?

Let's not forget F. de Saussure.
And Wittgenstein? Ludwig for sure!

Derrida as well would speculate,
as might Foucault about our fate.

We should mention too Edmund Husserl.
Could *he* decode this weird new world?

Barthes and Levinas: Both would weigh in—
with their own slants, their added spin.

We'd need more space on the long bookshelf
once each of these lads had relieved himself.

But at end of day, all done and said,
we'd be still vexed, still filled with dread.

A Load Off My Mind

On pg. 165 of Bruce Fink's *Clinical Introduction to Lacanian Psychotherapy*, we learn that "A number of contemporary American analysts seem to believe that perverts in therapy

are a dime a dozen, but when evaluated in terms of Lacanian criteria...the vast majority of people commonly referred to as perverts in fact turn out to be neurotics or psychotics." Phew! What a relief!

Eavan Boland, Rachel Maddow, and Me

Imagine my surprise when the famous Irish poet
Eavan Boland sat down at the table next to mine
while I was eating lunch in Newark, NJ—
an odd place for such an encounter, you might

be thinking, but the huge Dodge Poetry Festival
was in town, so that explains it, and also clarifies
why I was sure she was indeed Eavan Boland,
though I would've recognized her anyway

because there was no one in all the world
who looked even approximately as much
like Eavan Boland as Eavan Boland herself.
She was, like, absolutely Bolandian.

I was tempted to lean over, smile, and say, "Hey!
You're Eavan Boland!" But I refrained, because
I realized that she would probably reply, "Yes,
I am," and then I'd not know what to say next.

Last summer I was reminded of this long-ago
moment when the famous liberal political pundit
Rachel Maddow sat down at the table next to mine
while I was eating lunch—this time in Provincetown.

I recognized her right away, of course, and would've
anywhere because there is no one in all the world
who looks even approximately as much
like Rachel Maddow as Rachel Maddow herself.

She is, like, absolutely Maddovian.
I was tempted anew to lean over, smile, and say,
"Hey! You're Rachel Maddow!" But again
I held back, realizing that, like Eavan Boland,

she'd probably answer, "Yes, I am," and I'd
once more have to strain to extend the exchange,
and probably utter something really ridiculous,
maybe even something involving Eavan Boland,

whose name might mean nothing to Rachel Maddow,
despite her erudition. Famous poets, even the really
famous ones, are not well-known, after all, and
my weak attempt at witty repartee might have earned

only a quizzical frown from Rachel Maddow, or perhaps
a dismissive wave of the hand, as her lunches are no doubt
often interrupted by knuckleheads like me, who've watched her
on TV and want to claim, "I've met Rachel Maddow!"

So I'm really glad I said nothing this time too.
But maybe someday someone will lean over, smile,
and say, "Hey! You're George J. Searles, absolutely
Searlesian," not simply, "Please pass that ketchup."

Pulling the Rabbit Out of the Hat

Every once
in a while

you manage
to get it right,

wowing
the crowd,

astonishing
yourself.

II

The Poet's Primer
Lesson One: Subject Matter

Do not mention castles, vampires,
or any other gothic nonsense.
Why? Because—and I'm being gentle
here—such stuff is simply infantile.

Abstain from the broken heart's lament.
There's no way to be original
about it, or escape submersion
in quicksand swamps of self-indulgence.

Don't write about anyone writing.
(Do as I say, not as I'm doing.)
Religion is another no-no.
For the love of Christ, let's not go there.

So: Write no poem in which Dracula
gets a "Dear Count" letter from his girl
and decides to teethe on God instead.
Find some other point of reference. Please.

Next Thing on the To-Do List

Look at some vintage photographs and you'll see:
All of us—men and women alike—have become

much better looking during the past hundred years,
despite our grotesque piercings and ghastly tattoos.

Now let's work on getting a whole lot smarter,
starting at once, right away, today.

Fall Term

It breaks your heart, how downcast
these apple-cheeked young lovers look today,
slumped beneath the tree outside their dorm,

wearing fig leaves, baseball caps,
and "We're expelled" expressions
on their guilt-stained, sad-eyed faces.

They're history after only one semester,
and find themselves in a bad position
now forever. We're "old school" here

at Garden of Eden University.
The rules are the rules, by God;
there can be no readmission.

Shoptalk

Anyone who's ever worked
in a funeral home
can tell you stories.

Lots of them.

Like when the pallbearers
slipped on the frost-slick steps
and the coffin tumbled,

burst open.

That's a really good one...
the relatives' reactions,
the berserk daughter-in-law,

her melt-down,

her fistfight with the hearse driver,
the ensuing mêlée. All that.
But there are even better ones.

Way better.

Retirement

After thirty years or so
he decides to pack it in,
choke down the buffet dinner,
accept the phony gold wristwatch

and predictably kind words
from friends, quirky relatives,
and co-workers, even those
who didn't really like him.

Then he buys a doublewide
somewhere in the Sunshine State—
Daytona, Port St. Lucie,
or Fort Lauderdale, let's say,

or maybe Sarasota—
and straightaway drops stone dead,
face-down into his salad
(kale, most likely, or quinoa).

Not me. I'll never retire,
and so will live forever.
I'll keep showing up each day,
right here, punching the clock.

Governing Wisely

Breakfast cereal?
Far too many options—
a whole excessive aisle full,
shelf upon profligate shelf:

hot, cold, this kind, that kind,
enough different boxes on display
to feed a starving Third World village
for the next six months and a day.

Such glut can make you want to weep,
or collapse in crazed hilarity
right there on the supermarket floor,
and flop around like a suffocating fish.

After I've become King of North America,
invested with the ermine-trimmed robes,
ruby-studded crown, imperious queen,
randy royal concubines, and bulletproof Bentley,

my first supreme decree will be
to cut the morning menu down to size:
Cheerios, Corn Flakes, Raisin Bran,
Wheaties, and nothing more,

unless some clearly desperate supplicant
prostrate before the massive throne
makes a really good case
for our old pals Snap, Crackle, & Pop.

Double Standard

If she knows her stuff, any woman will finally overcome
whatever measure of resistance a man at first might offer.

How long it takes depends, of course, on chance and circumstance.
Being shipwrecked, for example, on a tiny desert island
(think *New Yorker* cartoon) would speed things up, we may assume.

But that is not to say there's any guarantee
that things will all work out the other way around.

Despite his best efforts, and regardless of the setting,
the man may not prevail. And if he fails, he fails completely.
Back to that little island. Imagine the poor guy's thoughts

as he stands there in his ragged shorts beneath the lone palm tree
watching the woman splash away, freestyling toward the circling fins.

It Ain't Over 'Til It's Over

I know, I know. Believe me: I know.
Your team's four runs in the hole,
losing to the mighty New York Yankees.

So you decide to bail, leave
during seventh-inning stretch, avoid
the traffic that will later clog the roads.

But this is not a good idea.
Have faith. Your guys might rally, come
from behind, load the bases, knot the score.

There's still the eighth and the ninth,
after all, and—if you get lucky—maybe
even a few big extra innings.

Workplaces From Hell

Taken verbatim from Treacy & Wiersema's *The Discipline of Market Leaders: Choose Your Customers, Narrow Your Focus, Dominate Your Market (Perseus Books, 1995)*, pg. 50.

Excellent companies run themselves
like the Marine Corps: The team is what counts,

not the individual....
The heroes...are the people who fit in....

These companies aren't looking for free spirits.
They want people who are trainable....

What's important is not who you are
but what the company will make out of you....

The best team player...will get his or her name
added to the plaque in the employee lunchroom....

The plaque itself—inexpensive...public—symbolizes much
about the company's culture....

Excellent companies can reward...employees
with an instant photo glued to that cheap plaque.

Smooth Talker

So I'm chatting up Jennifer Lopez's cousin—
this was in the Bronx, where I was working
at the time—and she tells me a story
about one night years ago
when she was at some downtown club

and this pushy, clearly wasted dude
lurched over and asked her to dance.
At first she said No, a *polite* No
(for starters, he was way too old for her),
but he kept asking and asking.

So finally they went out onto the floor.
The band was thrashing along,
the singer howling "God Save the Queen,"
when the guy grabbed his chest, turned blue,
and fell dead, right at her perfect Size 5 feet.

She says she still feels guilty about it
sometimes, that if she'd stuck to her guns
and shot him down, maybe he'd still be alive.
And she's starting to look pretty bummed out.
So, just to take things in a different direction

and lighten up the mood a bit, I tell her
that really she should be pretty proud of herself,
that not even J. Lo ever put a man into cardiac arrest
just by *dancing* with him: one more example
of how I always say the wrong damned thing.

Discretion

JoAnne, our always angry H.R. Director,
is sitting in the company cafeteria
eating a ham sandwich and waving one hand
back and forth in a doomed attempt to ward off

a relentless squadron of buzzing flies
when she asks what may or may not be
a rhetorical question. (It's actually a tough call.)
"Where do all these God-damned things *come* from?"

Whole screenloads of possibilities surge to mind
as if Googled: "Some are responsible, upstanding,
native-born American patriots, living and working
here in New York, JoAnne, just like you and me.

"Others, though, are undocumented immigrants,
living under assumed names and appalling conditions.
A small percentage are creatures from Outer Space,
posing as flies while they study me studying you.

"A few are from the Midwest, a couple more from Canada.
Those three over there, who won't meet your eyes,
may well be terrorists, contaminating your food and drink
with vile chemical agents whose effects you'll not detect

"until tomorrow or the day after, when it's too late....
Now *there's* something to think about, I guess.
Several more—God help them—are from New Jersey.
(At least they had the good sense to leave.)"

But I decide not to share these illuminations.
She's always disliked me, and her friend Cheryl once said
JoAnne had been raised in Secaucus, so that bit about Jersey,
in particular, would surely just make matters worse.

Adverse Reactions

If your doctor has prescribed this medication,
you may have questions about dosages,
possible side effects, and related concerns.
Be sure to read the label warnings and directions.

In particular, you should not work with power tools,
drive a motor vehicle, or operate heavy equipment
while taking this or other medications,
and you should not attempt a pedicure.

Do not ingest mind-altering substances,
except in moderation. Do not have sex
with more than five persons in one eight-hour period,
and never with more than three at once.

If you limit your consumption to two cases of beer
per day, you can expect no unexplained discomfort.
Likewise, smoking up to four packs of cigarettes
per day should produce no surprising contraindications.

But if you follow the news—t.v., print, or online—
you will almost certainly experience dizziness, nausea,
and a persistent sense of acute disorientation,
whether taking this medication or not.

In My Next Life: A Fantasy

That hulking bouncer in the horrid bar?
As Flaubert might say, *C'est moi!*

Once or twice a night I grab
some noisy little troublemaker

as if he were a wise-mouthed marionette,
run him headlong out the door,

and slam him on the frozen ground
beside somebody's rust-scarred car.

Then I stride right back inside,
pound down a beer, and strut around,

purposeful, businesslike,
my mouth shut tight,

with just the slightest hint
of an exasperated smile.

And everyone *tout de suite* becomes
a whole lot more well-mannered for a while.

The Fortuneteller's Bad Day

Madame Sofia peers into her crystal ball
with much the same theatrical display
of paranormal expertise as always,
but she's not herself this afternoon.

Along with her bangle bracelets, satin turban,
and cape festooned with cartoon moons,
shooting stars, and the planet Saturn,
she's wearing a frown and she looks beat,

like someone who's partied till sunup
but come to work anyway, against all odds.
"Sorry," she says, pocketing my twenty.
"I have a really bad headache, and nothing's clear.

As for the future, your guess is as good as mine."

His Master's Vice

Whenever I guide Jack to The Cataract Lounge,
a seedy "gentlemen's club" catering to the blind
and visually impaired, I always feel a little guilty.
As Jack's best friend, I really should tell him the truth:

that—like all the other old gents with their own dogs—
he's being ripped off. The dancers (well past their prime)
are wearing flannel shirts, bib overalls and beat-up Chucks,
and are hardly moving, just sort of shuffling in place

beside the neglected chrome pole on the stage
while the bored, superfluous bouncers stare at their phones.
But Jack and his geezer pals are clearly enjoying themselves,
tapping their white canes on the floor in time with the music

and shouting lewd blandishments at the unseen women.
So I don't want to spoil anyone's fun, Jack's least of all.

Death

It's always there, looming in the gloom
surrounding you, or—worse—looking
you right in the face, giving you what used
to be called a "hard stare," that hostile

glare from the neighborhood bully
right before he'd threaten to punch you out
or maybe skip the warning and go straight
to work, blackening your eye or perhaps

bloodying your nose. You'd live in fear
of his malevolent scowl and its dreaded
aftermath. Sure, there were ways to address
this situation, deal with it…placate

the thug by cringing or cowering, thereby
slaking his psychotic need to intimidate.
Or, if you were a little crazy yourself,
you could go all out, take him by surprise,

literally beat him to the punch, pound him
soundly in the snout and, if you were lucky,
cause him to reconsider and back off—
or, more likely, give you the thrashing

of your young life. Worthwhile nonetheless,
though, for then he'd never pick on you again,
preferring easier prey instead. But with The Reaper
there can be no appeasing, no fighting back.

My Cousin Vinny

A huge New York Yankees fan, both in his enthusiasm
for the Bronx Bombers and also in his imposing stature,
Vinny was hunkered down in front of the t.v. with a beer,
watching his team take on the hated Boston Red Sox,

when he was distracted by a commotion out in the street.
The Yanks were trailing, though they had two on and no outs,
so he was reluctant to tear his eyes away, but as the tumult
outside increased he decided to investigate, and rose to his feet.

The scene that greeted him when he looked out the window
was a reminder that some things are more important
than even baseball, and more worthy of his close attention.
On the sidewalk lay an overturned wheelchair,

and its owner, curled up beside it, was being tormented
by two thugs snarling cruel taunts, kicking him
with their bulky Timberland boots, and laughing.
Vinny did not approve. He picked up the Louisville Slugger

he kept in the corner next to the front door for whenever
it might be needed, and now it clearly was once more.
He stepped onto the porch, adroitly flipping the bat
from his right hand to his left and back again,

and addressed the louts, with an attention-getting salutation.
"Hey, you fuckin' scumbags," he barked, "Look at the man's
arms. If he could get up he'd beat the shit out of the both
of youse. But he can't get up, can he? So I guess

I'll just have to do it myself; y'know what I'm saying?"
The startled offenders looked up at Vinny and at the bat,
which subconsciously struck them as a big, thick, avenging
phallus (though not, most likely, in precisely those terms).

As Vinny approached the pair, they immediately turned
and ran, at a terrified full gallop, down the street, past the deli,
around the corner, and out of sight, like frantic mice
vanishing over the horizon in a vintage animated cartoon.

Progress

In *Genius*, James Gleick's best-selling biography
of legendary physicist Richard Feynman,
we discover that in 1950, cutting-edge experiments
revealed an interesting neutral pi meson

that would typically vanish after a lifetime
of a mere tenth of a millionth of a billionth
of a second, and this was considered fast
in those days. But Gleick adds that

standards were changing. Within a decade or so
tabulations would list this transient entity
in the STABLE column. Well, sure. We didn't
know nuthin' back in the '50s. Not like today.

Honest Abe

At the entrance to Jersey City's Lincoln Park
an impressively large statue of the president,
seated on a boulder atop a stone pedestal,
has greeted visitors since 1930.

Named "Mystic Lincoln," it depicts a somber,
pensive Abe, seemingly deep in troubling thoughts.
During my long-ago youth, every year on his birthday—
before there was a Presidents' Day—

we would honor the revered Rail Splitter
with a ceremony at the site, an ostensibly somber affair
featuring smarmy, self-serving presentations
by politicians, clergy, and other smug luminaries.

You'd think that African Americans would have attended
in large numbers, given their substantial presence
in the city, but they did not. No doubt they already knew
what the rest of us have since grudgingly learned,

that emancipation was largely just a political stratagem.
And of course they surely knew they would not be truly
welcome there, only reluctantly tolerated, condescended to,
as usual in Jersey City and elsewhere back in those days.

But the event organizers would always carefully recruit
one of the few Black Boy Scouts—invariably a small,
smiling, deferential kid who would carefully climb
the pedestal while encumbered with a large laurel wreath

he'd place around Abe's neck and then hop nimbly
back down, to restrained, patronizing applause.
And we'd all return home, feeling so much better
about ourselves, confident that there was really

not a racist bone in our whole collective body,
despite all stark evidence to the contrary
during each of the other 364 days of every year
(365 if it happened to be a leap year).

You Win Some, You Lose Some

Imagine poor Ralph's feelings—so conflicted
they must have been—when he heard
the news on his car radio about the Delta flight
he had angrily just missed because of a pileup
on the bottle-necked Cross Bronx Expressway
while he was rushing, late, to Kennedy:

plane down, engulfed in flames just minutes
after take-off; wreckage still smoldering;
all passengers and entire crew surely incinerated.
"Christ," Ralph intoned, then began to experience
a twinge of guilt about his relief—his dumb luck—
rather than sorrow at this harrowing loss of life.

In fairness, though, we are each always Numero Uno,
as far as every selfish one of us is really concerned,
so Ralph's reaction was nothing if not normal.
This world is home to countless other Ralphs
who've unwittingly escaped death because of failure
to catch flights that would've killed them, or who've
been favored in some other, oddly fortuitous way
despite related calamity for those around them.

But this Ralph's good fortune did not hold. He didn't see
the glistening dagger of ice hanging from the roof
of the convenience store he was entering later
that day, having paused for just a moment to snuff
out the remains of what would prove to be
his last cigarette, before that stalactite, melting
in the welcome winter sunshine, suddenly broke free,
fell, and pierced his skull, killing him instantly.

Another reminder (as if one more were needed)
of the arbitrary, impersonal nature of fate, the troubling
transience of life, the ongoing mystery of the human
misadventure, and—as a bonus—the dangers of tobacco.

The Golden Years

For the better part of your life, the predictable obituaries
in the morning paper don't claim much of your attention
as you skim along on your way to the petty-crime stories,
scandals, sports, Beetle Bailey, and good old Dagwood.

Sure, you briefly register the mug shots of the departed
crones and geezers, all much older than you and older
even than your parents, to judge by the wrinkled faces,
balding heads, dated eyeglasses, and WWII uniforms.

If by chance you read a few opening lines, you learn
that this one or that one passed away peacefully
in the downy comfort of their own bed, surrounded
by all their loved ones—if you can believe such claims.

Not to mention the old-timers borne aloft to Jesus
on the sturdy wings of radiant archangels and returned
to the embrace of departed parents, spouses, siblings,
and (let's not forget) cherished canine companions.

Clearly, some families and funeral homes are better
than others at concocting such reassuring fantasies,
giving the deceased far more colorful send-offs
than anything they may have enjoyed while alive.

All of this is easy to ignore, dismiss, or even ridicule
(not that you're so cold-hearted) as you turn the page
in search of news more aligned with your own concerns
in this life—thin as it is—rather than the next.

But at a certain point, when you're 60 or so, give or take,
things begin to change. You start to notice that many
of the dead are your contemporaries, or just a bit older,
and in some cases even younger by a few years or more.

Indeed, the obits, it suddenly seems, could now be mistaken
for a lightly edited page from your high school yearbook,
or maybe even from the book of the class who were freshmen,
mere pipsqueaks, when you were a lordly, immortal senior.

Resolutions

It was New Year's Eve again, but I had no date
and my friend Johnny—long dead now—was also
on his own that night, so we went to The Top Hat,
a decent little place on the other side of town,

and paid our $40 apiece and drank and ate and shot
the breeze until finally the ball dropped in Times Square
as everyone watched the t.v. and cheered and kissed
and Johnny and I started to feel like total losers

and got drunker and drunker, finally lurching outside
into a full-blown blizzard that had already nearly buried
my bald-tired little car, a troublesome two-seater
I'd bought from Butchie, my ex-girl's scary older brother.

We brushed off the windshield, got in, mushed along,
and decided to take a shortcut through the park
where—no surprise—we right away lost all control
and slid into a meadow filled with deep, immobilizing snow.

It wasn't easy to push the doors open, but we got out
and stood there, resigned to our plight and a long walk home
in the frigid night. Soon, though, this began to look like
the least of our problems when an old black Cadillac

full of young black men pulled up and the brothers got out
and advanced on us: silent, focused, businesslike.
They had no trouble at all lifting my car up, three on each
bumper, returning it to the road, wishing us a Happy New Year,

and sending us back on our way…back into the blinding whiteness.

III

Really Short Poems

At Sea

After you've been
under full sail awhile,

you start to tally up
how very many of your mates

have fallen overboard
or walked the plank.

You've clearly heard
each and every disconcerting splash.

Big Beefy Guys with Ponytails

There sure are
a whole lot
of those dudes.

Guitar Lessons

No young boy
ever learned
piano
or *French horn*
to meet girls.

How to Lose a Michelin Star

When George Donner called ahead
to make dinner reservations

nobody remembered to ask him
whether anyone in his Party

had any dietary restrictions.
A mistake, no matter how you slice it.

"If" is a Big Word

What goes around
comes around

if it's lucky enough
to still be moving at all.

Lieutenant Columbo's Wife

She was a lot like God:
Often mentioned,
but never seen;
maybe real,
maybe not.

Midnight

The big hand is nearly
on the 12.

And the little hand is almost
right straight up.

And the big hand is reaching
for your throat.

Mixed Blessing

On some days
life is so clear

you can see

all the way
to the bottom.

The Mouths of Babes

Why do infants cry so much?
Because they're smarter than they look,

and they know they have
their whole lives ahead of them.

No Pressure

Hey! Here it comes—
a femtosecond:

one millionth
of one billionth
of one second.

Don't blink,
or you'll miss the whole thing.

Overheard at the Diner

We'll never know.
That's the whole thing about it.

We'll never know.
We'll just. Never. *Know*.

Post Mortem

Do you remember what it was like,
waking up that first morning
after the funeral,

and suddenly remembering, and wishing
that it had all been just a dream, but realizing
that it was not, that it was all too real,

not a dream, but a nightmare, so to speak?

Three Questions

If not here,
Where?

If not now,
When?

If not you,
Who?

Willie, Mickey, & The Duke

Enough said?
Yes. Absolutely.
Enough said.

IV

Playground

Heat rising from the blacktop,
shimmering...

two rusted half-moon backboards,
rims askew...

off to the side, a seesaw,
a sandbox,

a slide, and five little swings,
motionless...

a high chainlink fence with its
gate padlocked.

Questions

Heard the one about the priest, the rabbi,
and the kangaroo who walk into a bar?
Yes? No? Can't remember?

When was the last time you kissed someone
(and meant it)? Last night? This morning?
Longer ago than that? How much longer?

Speaking of interpersonal dynamics,
when did you last get your ass kicked?
Back in high school, or more recently?

What would constitute a perfect day
for you? A perfect night? How about
a perfect life? A perfect death?

Tell me all the details; leave nothing out.
You've got to pull your weight here,
as the saying goes, and I'll pull mine.

Otherwise we'll not get to know
each other very well...not in depth.
Then again, do we really want to?

Escape from Jersey City

*We have one home, the first, and leave that one. / The having and
leaving go on together.* ~John Updike, "Shillington"

Under no circumstances whatsoever
should you allow yourself to be incarcerated,
hospitalized, joined in Holy Matrimony,
or otherwise detained in Jersey City.

For if you do, you'll almost surely vanish
sin noticio, like a political dissident
in the clutches of a bloodthirsty regime
and never be heard from again.

And, despite all efforts to learn your fate,
the only thing we'll ever know with any shred
of certainty will be that you were made to suffer
horribly before you died.

Semper Paratus

Hey, look: I was a Boy Scout in Jersey City
in the '50s, so wherever I find myself now
I always remember to look around and wonder,
"What is there here that would be a good weapon

if things go off the rails again?" And also,
"Where is the closest unlocked exit?"
Then I test that door, just to reassure myself,
so I can stop worrying, chill, relax a little.

Incentive

Rise and shine. Snap to. Strap on your jock.
Punch that clock. Confirm your many reservations.

Disappointing as your day today
will almost surely prove to be,

it still is yours and you must see it through
with something half akin to dignity.

Maybe, if you're lucky, once you're gone,
the committee will retire your number

and hang your threadbare jersey
near the faded banners overhead

beside old what's-his-name's
and whose-his-face's

and all the other ones up there, where someday
someone in the crowd might briefly glance,

though mostly out of boredom
or just by vagrant chance.

Civil Service

All you ever hear in the break room
at the Bureau of Death are complaints:
low pay, enormous caseloads, foul odors,
maddening software, crazy supervisors.

No way you can do the job right.
So what happens? You throw up
your hands, grind your teeth, soldier on,
short-shrifting the dead and soon-dead.

You know it's irresponsible; that they all
deserve better; that nothing's their fault;
that it's always been this way, always;
that before too long it'll be your turn to die.

But you can't help it. Like everyone here,
you finally get callous and resentful, cracking
juvenile, off-color gibes and groaners
as corpses keep arriving, arriving, arriving.

Higher Education

Brandee just got a part-time job
at the State U. branch campus here.
Next fall she'll teach an evening course:
"Funny Hats in Florentine Portraiture."

Her lucky break reminds me of my six years
as an undergrad at State. We learned so much:
our colors, our numbers, the alphabet,
the days of the week, the months of the year.

And that was only the first semester!
Later we began to read, add, subtract,
multiply, divide, tell time, and cross
the street unaccompanied by an advisor.

It was a whole new world.
The scales were peeled from our eyes,
the curtains drawn back to reveal
a stage loaded with illusions.

Since then the school has come a long way,
introducing a keyboarding major and hiring
a few faculty with actual M.A.'s, Ph.D.'s
and life experience in the correctional system.

And, as if on cue, the beer pong team went
all the way to the regional sub-finals this year,
and each player received a nifty blue windbreaker
and an impressive plastic trophy six inches tall.

Homage to Leon Golub, American Painter (1922-2004)

As long as rope and handguns are available,
victims will be tied to chairs and pistol-whipped
by snarling goons while cronies in makeshift uniforms

look on, smoking cigarettes and smiling cruelly.
Other hapless captives will cower on the ground,
and then, trussed up, be stomped to death.

Less fortunate ones will dangle from the rafters
upside down in straitjackets and be pumped
for information. In the alley, someone else,

perhaps already dead, will be stuffed into the trunk
of an idling black sedan, never to be seen again.
This is just the way things are all day and night

in Leon Golub's world, where anarchy prevails
and there seems to be no likelihood at all
that anyone will be restoring order soon.

So we should sit right down, have a nice hot cup
of tea and three delicious, chocolate-covered cookies,
and release a guilty, heartfelt sigh of gratitude

that Golub's reality, from which we cannot wrench
our anxious eyes away, bears such scant resemblance
to the one we occupy ourselves—at least for now.

Heartening Image

Feeling bad? Depressed?
Here's a little something
to cheer you up.

Picture your enemies, naked
as mottled med school cadavers,
fleeing through the public square,

shrieking as they're chased
around and around
the ornamental fountain

by muscular, whip-cracking,
indelicate ex-offenders (or current ones)
in chrome-plated Roman chariots

pulled by gargantuan wolfhounds
who have not had
their Kibbles yet today.

Misery Loves Company

Face it: Your life is ruined.
And not without reason.

You made eye contact on the streets of Manhattan,
wore your heart on your sleeve, led with your right,
pissed into the wind, and barked up the wrong tree.

You called in sick before a holiday,
leaped before you looked, kissed and told,
blew your own horn, and bit the hand that fed you.

You ordered meatloaf in a diner,
looked a gift horse in the mouth, let the cat out of the bag,
and counted your chickens before they were hatched.

You wore stripes with plaids,
didn't wear the shoe even though it fit, cried over spilled milk,
and threw the baby out with the bath water.

You sent cash through the mail,
took wooden nickels, spent it all in one place (bought a pig in a poke),
and tried to make a silk purse from a sow's ear.

You accepted a carry-on from an unknown person at the airport,
burned the candle at both ends, burned your bridges behind you,
and stayed in the kitchen even though you couldn't take the heat.

You did not remain seated until the aircraft had come
to a stop. You didn't shit, but stayed on the pot;
worse, you didn't wash hands before returning to work.

But don't feel bad.
The rest of us are every bit as much at fault as you,
and our lives are all quite ruined too.

Leave Well Enough Alone

Poor old Polanski must be revolving in his grave
like a big, plump chicken on a rotisserie spit,
now that his clueless son has sold the saloon
to a pair of slippery, smooth-talking Millennials

who—first big mistake—changed the name
from "Stanley's" to "The Maltese Falcon,"
then set about to gentrify the joint:
plants, chrome stools, plastic Tiffany lamps,

pub mirrors, high-tech jukebox, shit like that.
Even worse, a bunch of the shot & beer regulars
(volunteer firefighters, salt of the earth)
were informed they were no longer welcome

when wearing their barn clothes. "It's a turn-off,"
the new owners explained. This did not fly well.
How long will it take, I wonder, before the place
goes up in flames late some moonless winter night?

Everything's Under Control

You've gotta love the Salvation Army and its bell-ringers,
providing cheap used clothing and housewares
in their chock-full downtown thrift shop,
even if the place does smell like you-know-what.

While we're at it, let's have a big round of applause
for Catholic Charities with their impressive slate
of helpful services, all those Right to Life issues
and pedophilia scandals notwithstanding.

Put your hands together for the Rescue Mission,
serving up hot meals and earnest Christocentric counsel.
How about our friendly neighborhood bail bondsman?
(Ignore the cynics who say he's in it only for the money.)

Let's not forget the needle-exchange clinic, the AIDS Center,
Literacy Volunteers, the food pantry, the domestic abuse hotline,
and A.A. and their kissing cousins in Sexaholics Anonymous.
Just like the proverbial beat, the list goes on.

No matter what your problem is, or how bad things seem,
there's a program in place. Somebody's got you covered.
So rest easy. There's really nothing to worry about,
never been a better time to have your back to the wall.

Customer Service Has Its Limits

You want a nice BLT on white toast with a slice
of dill pickle, maybe, and a large coke? Coming right up!
A red-capped can of WD-40 or a
$19.95 Rid Advanced Removal System,
complete with miniature fine-toothed plastic comb, you say?
No problem. Any auto parts store will have the one,
my discreet neighborhood pharmacy the other.
I'll be right back with both.

You need a laminated, folding street map of Jersey City?
Tell you what I'll do: I'll send twenty bucks and a large SASE
to my man Sam at the Garden State News Store on Bergen Avenue,
have him mail the map to me, and tell him, "Keep the change!"
An official Skidmore College thong?
No problem at all. I'll go to the Web site,
click on "Store," order away. Maybe get one for myself while I'm at it.

A ball-peen hammer? I'm pretty sure there's one in the trunk of my car.
What's that? You'd like a well-organized, fully developed
500-750 word essay on Charlotte Perkins Gilman's
"The Yellow Wallpaper" for your English class
at Pontius Pilate Community College (PPCC)?
Jesus, what could be easier?
Forget AI. I'll bang one out for you tonight,
while watching that new PBS show,
Bad Bunny and Megan Thee Stallion Redecorate Downton Abbey.

A print copy of *The Boston Globe* or *The Poughkeepsie Journal*?
I can get you one, no sweat; it'll take four or five days, tops.
I'm here to serve, and your merest whim's my binding mandate.
Just don't hit me with any fussy orders, like, for example,
a clear statement of what love's got to do with it, got to do with it,
or where time lands after it flies, or why it flies or lands at all.

Cultural Differences

It's easy to find fault with how we live
in this country, killing half our time glued,

as the saying goes, to the television,
watching a bizarre array of extreme sports

and equally pointless conventional ones,
and wasting the other half scanning our phones

in garish shopping malls as big as baronies—
faux villages with junk food franchises,

private security squads, and valet parking
for the luxury sedans, racy coupes, and SUVs.

Elsewhere in the world, life's song is played
in a simpler, less extravagant key.

People go about their business
in a more purposeful, down-to-earth sort of way,

uncorrupted by excess, alertly scurrying
from place to ruined place in a wary semi-crouch

while trucks explode at curbside and bullets ricochet
off buildings and splash on pavement stones.

Science

I learned two new facts today,
one of them good news,
the other bad.

First, the good news:
Recent studies have shown
that alcohol consumption
inhibits the production
of fibrogen,
a blood-clotting protein,
thus reducing the risk
of heart disease and stroke.

Now for the flip side:
We share 98.4% of our genome
with chimps, 95% with dogs,
and 57% with flatworms.

There's probably a connection
here somewhere,
but it would take a bartender
to really explain it.

Coming Soon: Suspended Sentence,
Anger Management Class

Yesterday my ex-wife was beaten up again
by her other ex-husband, whom I've never liked.
No broken bones this time, but some nasty bruises.

Today I'll visit my favorite local hardware store,
have them cut me a nice, eighteen-inch length of lead pipe,
and friction-tape one end, for a slip-proof grip.
Then I'll contemplate my ex's second ex, to create focus.

Tomorrow I'll visit him. We'll chat—just the two of us—
and I'll explain in great detail why I've never liked him.
At first he won't pay much attention, but then he will.

Missing

The half-clothed corpse is finally found,
sprawled beneath a sheet
of plywood in a trash-strewn lane
behind the old, abandoned factory.

It's come upon by two young boys
on bicycles, searching for a lost pup,
a white one with brown spots,
gone now for three long days.

In a sense, the kids get more
than they bargained for. But after the fuss
dies down, they're disappointed anyway;
the dog never does turn up.

On Good Authority

It's right there in the Book of Leviticus:
"Nothing's lousier than a really lousy pizza."
Or was that Plotinus? Or perhaps Spinoza?
Now that it's come up, I'm not sure.
It could easily have been Pliny the Elder.

Or, for that matter, Pliny the Younger...
or even one of the Holbeins, to stretch a point.
Then there's that old chestnut, "Don't get your meat
where you get your bread." That was Duns Scotus,
if I'm not mistaken. Or maybe Carlyle...or James.

"James who?" I once heard someone ask.
It's a fair question, but I'm getting off the track,
like the little engine—not the famous one
who said he could, but that other one
(his name escapes me now),

the one who wouldn't stay on the rails
because he wanted to romp among the flowers
in the field. That's pretty far-fetched,
when you really stop to think about it...
not to mention the whole idea

of a gendered locomotive to begin with.
In any case, he should've known better.
We're not supposed to stray off course,
but should always hew to the line,
through thick and thin, come hell or high water.

Like poor old Sisyphus in the Greek myth
about the boulder and the mountain
and all that damned pushing, pushing, pushing,
forever and ever and ever.
Sisyphus? Yes, I'm sure about that one.

Selective Enforcement

When two women fistfight in the parking lot
of a rowdy roadhouse or an all-night greasy spoon,
and the police show up, there are tears and F-bombs,
but no one ever seems to get arrested—unless, of course,

gentlemen nearby, energized by witnessing the fray,
become involved themselves, launching their own foray
into the sweet science...breaking bones, drawing blood.
Only then do the cops decree the gloves are truly off.

False Advertising

Alongside many of the nation's thoroughfares
stand large, infield-shaped yellow signs depicting
graceful, leaping deer—each buck with its head up,
front legs bent and lifted high in the air

as if confidently clearing a hurdle
in some fanciful track & field competition.
But this is plainly yet another sobering case
of cheery fiction versus cruel reality.

Most of the deer that I observe during my commute
are all quite still, sprawled on the shoulder of the road
in grim, terminal repose, their four fragile limbs
splayed at awkward, disturbing angles.

Sherry A., Iowa

Those little, inch-square Dove candies
never fail to satisfy my craving
for a sweet treat that's quick to eat.
And each one comes with a bonus:

a signed greeting printed on the inside
of the red foil wrapper.
Like the sayings in the fortune cookies
included with my order of lo mein

or pork fried rice, these Dove messages—
sent to the company, or so it seems,
by chocolate-lovers around the country—
vary greatly in their wisdom and utility.

The one I'm reading now, for instance,
is especially tough to measure. No way
to know for sure if it's good advice or not,
an encouraging thought or a disturbing one.

"Smile, someone is thinking of you!"
Sherry A. instructs me all the way from Iowa,
a state I've never visited, and likely never will.
But her admonition has gotten me thinking.

Plenty old by now, I've known a long, pied parade
of people during the course of this puzzling life,
so I may well, in fact, be in the thoughts today
of someone from the past, or even the present.

But I'm not certain this is cause to smile.
Maybe, maybe not. I fear the odds may be no better
than 50/50. It depends on who's doing the thinking.
Yes, it depends. It *all* does, Sherry A., always.

Back in the 20th Century We Kept Ourselves Pretty Busy

looking at blackbirds thirteen ways,
placing jars in Tennessee, and calling the rollers
of big cigars. We went without the meat
and cursed the bread. We woke to black flak
and the nightmare fighters. We slouched

toward Bethlehem, put our queer shoulders
to the wheel, and took the road less traveled by.
That made all the difference. Year after year,
April was the cruelest month, so we let the fish go
and dragged ourselves through the negro streets at dawn

looking for an angry fix. Constantly risking absurdity,
we leaned on the john door in the 5 Spot, wishing
we were in Paterson, or on the avenue bearing the initial
of Christ into the new world, closer to The Bridge.
Because we were always talking, we dove into the wreck,

lay down in a hammock at William Duffy's farm
in Pine Island, Minnesota, and wasted our lives.
We did it exceptionally well; we did it so it felt like hell.
Our minds were not right; we ourselves were hell.
Yes, those were the (houseboat) days!

We watched our L=A=N=G=U=A=G=E,
asked questions about angels, and celebrated
hips, uteruses, and the Pope's penis.
Though we knew women, lovely in their bones,
there sat down once a thing so heavy on our hearts,

Daddy, that we had to kill you. Finally we left school,
lurked late, struck straight, sang sin, thinned gin,
jazzed June, and died soon; we'd had a death
sentence we'd spent all our lives appealing.
We did not go gentle into that good night.

George J. Searles is a SUNY Distinguished Teaching Professor of English and Latin at Mohawk Valley Community College (Utica NY). He has also taught creative writing on the upstate campus of Pratt Institute (Brooklyn) and graduate courses for The New School (NYC). Widely-published (literary criticism, journalism, textbooks, poetry), he is a former Carnegie Foundation "Professor of the Year" and is currently editor of *Glimpse*, a poetry annual.